A JUST FOR A DAY BOOK

WINTER WHALE

JOANNE RYDER

ILLUSTRATED BY
MICHAEL ROTHMAN

A MULBERRY PAPERBACK BOOK / NEW YORK

Special thanks to Dr. Paul Forestell, Director of Research and Education, Pacific Whale Foundation in Maui, Hawaii, for his expert reading of this manuscript.

AUTHOR'S NOTE

Playful acrobats, singers, and wanderers, humpback whales spend much of their lives hidden underwater. These large yet graceful marine mammals live in all the oceans of the world. Natural athletes, they often leap above the waves, breaching again and again. Like humans, they compose and sing complex songs, songs that change from year to year.

Scientifically known as *Megaptera novaeangliae*, humpback whales get their common name from the way their backs hump as they dive. They have very long, winglike flippers and wartlike bumps on their heads. Each humpback has distinctive markings, especially on its tail flukes. These markings enable scientists to identify and study individual whales as they wander through the world's seas.

Many humpback whales migrate thousands of miles each year. They spend the summer feeding in polar seas on schools of small fish and on shrimplike krill, which thrive in cold waters. A humpback may eat a ton of food each day. Its mouth is a huge strainer. As a humpback gulps water, food is caught in the fringed baleen that hang from the whale's upper jaw.

After feeding all summer, many humpbacks journey far to spend the winter in tropical waters. There, off the shores of the Hawaiian Islands, the West Indies, and other tropical lands, they gather to mate, to bear their calves, and to sing their famous warm-water songs.

The long, haunting songs of adult male humpbacks may attract females and keep other singers at a distance. A male sings alone with his head down. His song may be heard for several miles underwater. At the start of the winter, the whales in an area sing the same song. Gradually, singers add, drop, or vary themes. By winter's end, the song they are singing has evolved into one quite new and different. This new song is the one they will all begin singing when they return to the tropical seas the following winter.

The whale whose day is described in this book is one of these winter singers, an adult male humpback swimming near the Hawaiian Islands.

Acrylic paint was used for the full-color artwork. The text type is 14 point ITC Garamond Book.

Printed in the United States of America.
3 5 7 9 10 8 6 4 2

The Library of Congress has cataloged the Morrow Junior Books edition of *Winter Whale* as follows:

Ryder, Joanne. Winter whale / Joanne Ryder; illustrated by Michael Rothman. p. cm. —(A Just for a day book)
Summary: Transformed into a humpback whale, a child experiences life in the ocean among other whales.
ISBN 0-688-07176-7 (trade).—ISBN O-688-07177-5 (library) [1. Humpback whale—Fiction. 2. Whales—Fiction.]
I. Rothman, Michael ill. II. Title. III. Series. PZ7.R959Th 1991[E]—dc20 90-19174 CIP AC

First Mulberry edition, 1994.
ISBN 0-688-13110-7

One gray morning
rain whispers,
waking you, calling you.
Run outside
and feel the warm rain
slide over your arms,
run down your face
and into your open mouth.

You are a rainy thing now,
slippery and wet all over.
You stretch out your arms
and feel them changing,
feel yourself growing
in the gentle rain
that surrounds you—
then changes too
into the wide deep sea.

You are large and grand,
swimming through
an ever-changing, ever-moving world.
All around you,
small ones are swimming, too.
Bend your long strong tail
up and down, up and down.
Feel yourself gliding forward,
flowing through the warm salty waters,
powerful whale.

As you swim, you stretch
your long, long flippers,
bending, moving, turning them
so you can slide
        right
    and left
       and even upside down.
As graceful as a bird
flying through the empty sky,
you soar through the sea,
graceful whale.

Below you, there is darkness.
Above you, there is brightness.
Swim up toward the sparkling lights
as spotted fish dart this way
and striped fish dash that way.

You glide up,
up into the sky
and breathe out—
                    Whooosh!
A fine white mist
sprays up high
from blowholes on your head.
Take a deep breath now
and feel the clean fresh air
rush through your blowholes
into your big chest…. Ahhh!

Now push,
push yourself down.
Your long back bends
in a hump as you dive.
Your strong wide tail flukes
flash white in the sunlight
as you plunge straight down
among long sunbeams
lighting your way
into the sea.

You are a humpback whale,
gliding up and down
between your two worlds—
of sea and sky, of water and air.

In the warm waters,
other whales gather.
Swimming together,
you are a pod of whales,
your breaths rising
like towers of white mist
against the green hills, the blue sky.

A new calf swims slowly
through the warm waters,
his mother beneath him
guiding him, touching him.

All winter long
he will drink her rich milk.
All winter long
he will nurse and grow.
Yet his mother will fast,
like all grown humpback whales,
not eating till summer
when they swim to the north,
to the cold-water seas
rich with food they will catch
in their wide-open mouths.
But today her wide mouth
is closed, just like yours.

Underwater,
the sea is full of sounds—
the soft sounds
of water swirling, dolphins calling.
Far away, miles away,
someone is singing
alone in the sea.
You listen, knowing
this warm-water song.
And your head sinks low,
as you sing the song too.

Near and far,
other whales listen.
Whales swimming together
and mothers and calves
hear your long song
that drifts through the water.
New singers,
male whales
far apart and alone,
begin singing too,
till the wide sea hums
with your warm-water song.

You are a humpback whale
in a warm-water sea,
singing your song,
holding your breath
till, at last,
you soar up and up
through the blueness.

You leap high into brightness,
waving your long, long flippers,
crashing and splashing,
making your own waves.
For one moment
you are a leaping whale
soaring from the sea to the sky.

As day ends, you swim
in a world of blackness
above and below.
Clouds swirl
over your head,
bringing rain
that falls,
that trickles
down your bumpy face,
your bumpy chin,
changing you again....

Gently, you float
to shallow water
where your small toes
touch the sand.
Standing tall,
you run through the darkness
to bright lights and supper.

And as you run, you hum
a warm-water song
that glides through the night
like the whales in the sea.